Rapture

Helen V. Alexander

ISBN 1977515908
ISBN-13: 978-1977515902

www.helenalexanderministries.com

DEDICATION

This book is dedicated to God and my son, Troy
Alexander. I am forever grateful to the Lord. Troy has
been my best friend for many years; he has loved God
since his childhood years. As a result of his commitment to
Christ, I am able to enjoy my life as a parent.

Chapter One

My Love for the Lord

I was born in a Southern town in a dedicated Christian home. I remember very clearly many things from my childhood days. I well recall that when I was eight years of age, I would listen to a local Christian radio station. My favorite show was the Bible Quiz. The host of the daily radio show would ask several biblical questions. The public was given the opportunity to call the radio station and give the correct answers. The winner would receive a prize. I began to read the Bible because I wanted to win.

On several occasions, I was the recipient of the award. That gave me great happiness. I was grateful for the times when I didn't win because that encouraged me to study the Bible.

Dreams and Revelations

When I was a teenager, I discovered that things that I dreamed would eventually become a reality. One night I dreamed that I sat on my sunglasses and broke them. The next day, my husband and I were getting ready to travel. I got in the car, sat down, and heard a loud cracking noise. I discovered that I had broken my sunglasses. The dream came true. At that time, I was going to church on a regular basis, but I was not saved. After I became a spirit-filled believer, I realized that God was dealing with me during the period of time when I didn't know Him as my Savior. I was amazed at the things that He revealed to me. After the Lord saved me, He revealed to me the following scripture: "For the gifts and calling of God are without repentance" (Rom. 11:29). Then I understood that I could have a gift from God and at the same time not know him as my personal Savior.

There are many people that have gifts from God but they are not using them to glorify Him. God has no respect of persons. All good and perfect gifts come from Him but He allows us to choose to use them for His glory or use them for the works of Satan. Unfortunately, many people have chosen to use their gifts for Satan and self-gain.

Getting My Attention

It is not the will of God that any of us should perish but that we should all come to the knowledge of the truth. God's Spirit will draw us to Him but it's up to us to accept Him. I have always enjoyed listening to gospel groups. One night I decided to visit a church that was having a concert featuring one of my favorite groups. As the group was singing, suddenly I felt something hit me in the back of my head. I had a feeling as though I had been hit with a baseball bat. I grabbed my head, jumped up out of my seat and ran out of the sanctuary. My two sisters were with me and they followed. I didn't know what had happened. My sisters asked me, "What's the matter?" I had a difficult time trying to explain to them that I had been hit in the back of the head. Of course, they didn't understand that because they were sitting right next to me and had not seen or heard anything. When I became a Christian, the Lord brought that experience back to my memory. At the time of that incident, He was trying to get my attention.

I recall well hearing my father pray during the early hours of the morning. I heard Him when he asked God to take care of his children. It was the prayers of my parents that kept me from death. Satan tried to destroy me but God said "no"!

Chapter Two

The Miracle

In 1971, the Lord worked a miracle for my son, Troy, and me. I was pregnant with Troy at the time. As the time of delivery drew closer, I developed a serious illness known as Toxemia – blood poisoning. My blood pressure was extremely high. The doctor said that if I had stubbed my toe against something, I probably would have died. Serious physical problems seemed to be mounting. Before Troy was born, several x-rays were taken. The results indicated that his head looked like what is called a "water head" and that it was very large. I was told that he would be deformed.

My family was warned of the possibility that one of us would not survive the delivery. I had no knowledge of that. I was not given any medicine during the delivery. I recall seeing the doctor and nurse standing by my bedside. I'm sure they were amazed that both of us survived. My blood pressure was extremely high after the delivery. A medical team watched me very closely. Through much prayer, Troy and I received a miracle from God.

When Troy was born, he was "coughing" very hard and appeared to be choking. The doctors ran many tests on him. All of the results were negative. My doctor suggested that I undergo several tests. The results indicated that I had a tumor on my thyroid, half of which had to be removed. God used my son's discomfort while choking to draw attention to the fact that there was a problem in the midst. He's so awesome! I remember being taken into a room by a medical assistant where something that looked like a large tube was placed over my neck. As the medical assistant looked into the medical equipment that had been placed over my throat, he became very excited and told the

3

nurse to call my doctor right away. Of course, that reaction caused me to become fearful. Later the doctor arrived and I was told that the tumor that was in my throat was too large to be removed at that time. I was placed on medication and I was allowed to go home with my newborn son.

A month later, I returned to have the surgery. God performed a miracle. It was a very serious operation. The doctor was an excellent surgeon. The incision left a very thin scar that could easily be covered with something as thin as a piece of thread. Almighty God guided the surgeon's hand, eliminating the chance of my having to live with a scar that would not be pleasing to the eye. God is so awesome.

Chapter Three

Seeking God

I attended a local church for many years. The preacher was the only person that brought a Bible to church on a regular basis. He would read a scripture and expound on it. At that time, I didn't realize that salvation is not based upon what you hear but rather having a personal relationship with Jesus Christ. In 1980, I began to seek the Lord with all of my heart. I attended many churches, searching for something to fill that void that was in my spirit.

A friend invited me to attend a Wednesday night service that was being held at her church, which was located in South Jersey. When we arrived, the sanctuary was filled with people. Everyone seemed to be very happy. Their faces were full of smiles. I wanted that happiness that I saw being expressed. The praise service was awesome. At the end of the service, the minister gave the altar call and asked if there was anyone in the congregation that wanted to be filled with God's Spirit. He said, "Get up out of your seat and come to the altar now." Immediately, my younger sister and I walked down the aisle. I did not know what he meant by "being filled with God's Spirit." But I said to myself, "If this is of God, I want it!" There were about seven people at the altar. The pastor of that church began to pray for us and God filled us with His Spirit. I had never experienced such joy. Jesus Christ is joy unspeakable!

I was what one would call "plain Jane." My older sister was very smart, very intelligent. My younger sister was very pretty. So there were many times when my heart was saddened because I didn't get the attention from others that my sisters received. My parents were wonderful, God-fearing people. They showed a lot of love to all of their children. They made me feel very special. This unspeakable joy of Christ that was now living inside of me made me feel extra special. For the first time in my life, all of the insecure feelings disappeared. I realized that I didn't have to be brilliant nor did I have to be pretty to feel loved. I discovered that "one with Jesus" is a majority. He is joy unspeakable and full of glory. He gave me a peace that I had never had before. I discovered that, naturally speaking, I could have peace in the midst of storms because of Jesus!

God is intelligent. He created intelligence. He'll make us intelligent because He knows everything. The Lord is wonderful. His works are beautiful. Look at His creation - consider the lilies. They are the work of His hands. They are beautiful and we can be just as beautiful spiritually! The Lord said that He would beautify the meek with salvation. All we have to do is humble ourselves.

The Turning Point

Visiting my friend's church was the turning point in my life. The church was quite a distance from where I lived. I knew that it would require some searching to find a church that believed in being filled with the Spirit of God. There were many churches around but most of them were "quiet" churches. I needed the anointing to feed the Spirit that was now inside of me. The anointing of God is a power that I did not know existed.

Food for the Soul

One summer day, I was listening to the radio and I heard a preacher expounding on the word of God. He was preaching with the power of God that comes with the anointing! It was as if I was sitting at the table enjoying a delicious meal. My soul was fed with spiritual manna from on high. God knew that my soul needed to be nourished. He knows just what we need. He promised not to leave us or forsake us and He will supply all of our needs. "But my God shall supply all of your need according to his riches in glory by Christ Jesus" (Phillip. 4:19).

I continued to listen to that radio program for a period of one year. It was a fifteen-minute daily broadcast from Monday through Friday. During the week, I had a daily fifteen-minute meal to which a sirloin steak could never compare. On Saturdays and Sundays, I suffered from spiritual malnutrition because I could not find a local church that worshiped God in the fullness of His power.

Chapter Four

News About the Rapture

One night, I decided to visit a church in North Jersey. I had heard the Pastor of the church on the radio so I was inspired by the Lord to visit. Upon my arrival, I saw a very small church that was located in a residential area. As I walked into the building, I noticed that there were many young and adult people there. The anointing of God was very thick. You could feel God's presence upon entering the building. There was a very warm feeling inside of the sanctuary. I sat on the last pew in the church. The people were singing and worshipping God. His anointing filled the place. I noticed a newsletter on the pew. I picked it up and began to read it. Across the top of the page was written these words: "Are you ready for the Rapture?" At that time, I didn't know anything about the Rapture. I didn't know the meaning of the word "Rapture". Although I had attended church faithfully, I had never heard anyone mention the word "Rapture." I put the newsletter in my handbag and focused on the worship service.

During the following week, I decided to read the newsletter in its entirety. The article briefly mentioned the coming of the Lord and gave some scriptures as reference. I began to read the Bible everyday. Something inside of me was inspiring me to search the scriptures with urgency. I spent hours reading the Word. Sometimes on Saturdays I would spend the entire day searching the scriptures for details about the Rapture. My search was not just an effort to gain knowledge about the Rapture but also to enable me to share that knowledge with others. I had no idea that some day Jesus will appear in mid-air to meet the believers. I must admit that as I searched the scriptures, I was frightened by all of the things that I discovered that will be happening on the earth after the Rapture.

I am convinced through the study of the bible, that it is important for me to be caught up to meet the Lord in mid-air – to be "Raptured", so that I won't have to go through the terrible Tribulation Period that will take place afterwards. I felt the urgency to share this information with as many people as I could reach.

Chapter Five

The Test

God began to reveal things to me. I was on my way home from work one day and as I drove across the railroad tracks, suddenly my son's face appeared before me in a vision. It appeared to be covered with blood. I became very nervous and I began to drive the car faster. The enemy made me think that the worst thing in the world had happened to my son. When I got home, I found that my son was safe and everything seemed just fine.

I had a prayer room in my house, which I used on a daily basis specifically for Bible reading and prayer. God's anointing filled that room. His presence was so awesome. I recall sitting in that prayer room one evening. It was the same day that I saw in a vision my son's face filled with blood. I was reading the Bible when I heard a voice say, "Get out of the house." I couldn't understand the command. I was a new Christian and was not always sure whether I was hearing the voice of the Lord or imagining things.

I was home alone with my son and he was sleeping. Again I heard a voice say, "Get out of the house." I continued to read the Bible. I asked myself, "Why should I get out of the house?" Suddenly, I broke out in a sweat and a nervous feeling came over me. Again I heard a voice say, "Get out of the house." Immediately, I awakened my son. We packed up our things and drove to my parents' home to spend the night.

About 2:00 a.m. the next morning, I got a telephone message that my home had been burglarized. Many things went through my mind as I drove towards my home. I was thinking of the greatness of God and how mighty He is!

He's awake when we're sleeping so He sees all things. "Behold he that keepeth Israel shall neither slumber nor sleep" (Psa. 121:4-5). The Lord is thy keeper! When I arrived home, I noticed that there was a ladder that had been placed against the house that reached up to my son's bedroom. The window had been broken. The intruders entered the house through that window. Then my mind flashed back to my experience earlier in the day when I was driving home from work and I saw my son's face in the vision.

God is awesome and He will not leave His people in the dark. He'll warn us before the storm arises. Many of the windows in the house had been broken and a lot of valuables had been stolen.

When I walked into the prayer room in the house, I noticed that one of the desk drawers had been pulled open but nothing else had been touched. It was obvious that when the intruders entered that room, God's anointing overpowered them. It appeared as though they left in a hurry. God's anointing will break every yoke. I thank God that He warned me to leave the house. Because God knows everything, he saw the enemy's plan. It is true, "No weapon that is formed against thee shall prosper" (Isa. 54:17).

I have thought about that experience often. I've also asked myself many questions about it: What would have happened to us if we had stayed in the house? How would I have reacted? Would I have panicked? Would I have slipped into shock and left my son at the mercy of the intruders? You may find yourself in a difficult situation without any directions. If you have a personal relationship with Christ, you don't have to worry. He will make things happen for you. He caused a great sweat to drench my body to let me know that He meant, "Get out of the house," and that it was urgent for me to do so. "In all thy ways acknowledge him, and he shall direct thy paths" (Prov. 3:6).

I continued to go back to that prayer room, and I spent many hours studying scriptures that relate to the Rapture. I was determined to learn everything I could about the Lord's coming. During that time, I had some very difficult experiences.

Chapter Six

More Tests

One Sunday, my mom and dad invited the family over for dinner. We had a wonderful fellowship. It was always a pleasure to be in my parents' presence. They loved the Lord. They taught all of their children to reverence the Lord and to obey his commandments. As I was leaving their home, I raised my foot to step down to the next step on the porch and immediately I felt an excruciating pain in the right side of my body. I thought that I would not be able to take another step because of the severity of the pain. I had no idea of the horrible experience that awaited me.

I was taken to a nearby hospital. As I entered the hospital, it seemed as though no one would give me any attention. Finally, I was taken into the emergency room and escorted into a room where I was left (in pain) for about one-half hour. Later a nurse came in to see me. She was very mean and had no compassion for me. I was told to climb up on the bed. I was in a lot of pain but I managed to follow her instructions without any assistance from her. She then left the room. I waited another half-hour without seeing anyone on the medical team in the emergency room. I decided to leave and go to another hospital, especially since it seemed that no one was going to be taking care of me soon.

I suffered greatly, but I managed to drag myself past the nurses' station. I looked into the faces of the nurses and the doctors. All of their faces looked like demons. They stared at me with hatred. I could feel the presence of hatred as I passed them. Of course I didn't understand that at that moment but as I continued to study God's word, I later understood that demons will be ruling the

13

land during the reign of the Antichrist. If you do not have the mark of the Beast on your forehead or on your right hand, life will be very difficult. You won't be able to get any help. I'll discuss this later in the book.

I was taken to another hospital about five miles away. When I entered the hospital, I went through the necessary procedures and was taken into the emergency room. Upon my arrival there, I was asked to sit on the bed and I was told that the nurse would be in to see me shortly. When she appeared, she had a beautiful glow on her face. I felt that God had sent His angel to rescue me. The nurse asked, "What's the matter?" Immediately, the excruciating pain left my body. It seemed as though the nurse was filled with the presence of God. I thought, surely a light had come to fill the darkness. I sat up and told the nurse that the pain was gone and that I didn't feel that I needed further assistance. I left that hospital without being treated. At that time, I did not understand what I was going through. But, as the Lord began to reveal the book of Revelation to me, it became very clear to me that the Lord was preparing me to write a musical play entitled Raptured/Left Behind.

I've experienced some of the pain that people will feel if they are left behind and don't make the Rapture. Therefore, I can declare, without any reservations, that there will be awful times on the earth during the Tribulation Period.

Chapter Seven

The Fire

God has a way of showing us His power to increase our faith. It takes a lot of faith to do a work for God. The enemy plots against the believer but our faith will make us successful. One summer night, I was anointing my doors before going to bed and I heard the Lord say, "The anointing will keep them out." At that moment, I thought that someone was going to try to break into the house. I was hoping that I wouldn't be home when that happened and yet I knew that God sees all things.

The next day, I was on my way home from work and as I turned the corner, I could see smoke, fire trucks and a lot of people standing around. As I looked toward my home, I could see smoke pouring out of the windows from the apartment above mine. Amazingly, I did not get excited. God will give you peace in the midst of your storms. As I got closer to the house, I saw my son standing outside. He also seemed to be very calm. Later, I found out that the calmness that God gives us serves as a testimony of His power. My neighbor could not understand why I was not upset.

The apartment above mine was so badly damaged that the tenants could not live there. My son and I were allowed to go inside later to see the damage. The firemen used a lot of water to extinguish the fire. Amazingly, God had caused all of the water from the apartment above to flow to the center of the ceiling in my living room. The ceiling cracked in the middle and the water dropped in the middle of the floor. None of my furniture was damaged. Only the carpet needed to be replaced. We were told that we could not stay in the apartment that night but that we could come back the next day and pick up the personal things that we would need.

The next day, we went to the house with the firemen for what we thought would be a short visit to pick up our clothes. What an amazing experience that was. None of our clothing smelled like smoke. The fireman tested the outlets and found them to be completely dry. He said, "I've never seen anything like this." The Lord reminded me of His words, "The anointing will keep them out." God's anointing kept the flames from destroying my home. We were allowed to go back into the house that same day and we continued with our lives as usual. The only thing we were missing was carpet on the living room floor. God is awesome!

Later, I was allowed to see my neighbor's apartment, which was located directly above mine. I noticed that the thermostat had melted against the wall. The tiles on the kitchen floor were completed burned. My neighbor's kitchen was located directly above mine but I didn't have any damage in my kitchen. God is a mighty God! He's awesome!

Chapter Eight

Ten Days of Adventure with Jesus, The Devil and his demons

On July 12, 1996, I went to the hospital because I was in a lot of pain. I was given a prescription and sent home. Tuesday, July 16th, I was having severe stomach pains. I said to the Lord, "If there is something seriously wrong with me, please show me a sign." At that moment, I felt something like a dagger pierce me in the middle of my stomach. Immediately, I returned to the hospital.

July 16, 1996 was the beginning of ten days of adventure that I will never forget. I was admitted to the hospital. I was examined and told that I would have to have surgery immediately. The nurse that was supposed to pre-op me was being controlled by a demon. She said to the medical assistant, "I am not going to medicate her. They will do that when she arrives upstairs." I watched her as she placed my pre-op medication (needle) in her pocket. Immediately Satan sent thoughts through my mind of undergoing surgery without that medication. God will never fail. He had my son, Troy, right there. He was allowed to go upstairs to the operating room entrance with me and, in fact, he was given a cap to cover his head. He was then able to tell the doctor that I had not been medicated.

There is no need to worry about anything. God will step in on time. "God is not a man that he should lie. Hath He said and shall He not do it?" (Num. 23:19).

Demons Are Real

The night after the operation, the devil and his demons came to visit me. Spiritually, I watched as a woman I recognized walked into my room and sat down beside me. She then pointed a gun at my face. A strong power immediately pointed my finger at the woman and said, "By the power that Jesus Christ has put inside of me, you go. Go!" She looked up and it appeared that she had lost her sight and she began to try to feel her way out of my room.

Immediately, a second woman that I recognized but who is no longer living walked into my room. As she sat down, I repeated those words, "By the power that Jesus Christ has put inside of me, you go. Go!" She, like the first demon, looked upward and seemed to have lost her sight. Then she proceeded to leave the room. At that time, I heard a voice that sounded like rolling thunder, which said, "No weapon that is formed against you shall prosper."

I then returned to an alert state and I began to wonder what my roommate was thinking. I was hoping that she had not heard the conversation that had taken place. I positioned myself in the bed so that I could see her. Apparently she had not heard anything. I was glad that she had not witnessed my encounter with the demons. Demons are real! But, so is God!

I questioned God about the dead and the living women that I had seen. He said, "No weapon neither past nor present that is formed against you shall prosper." My final night in the hospital will be a night that I will never forget. Spiritually, I was taken to a place where everything looked spotless. My eyes had never beheld such beauty before that night.

When I arrived, I saw all kinds of beautiful jewels. As I tried to pick them up, they slipped right through my hands. It reminded me of gold being processed. The color of the jewels was gold but they were like a silvery, slippery gold. As I touched them, they just seemed to float. The surface of the floor was pure gold. It was so pure looking that if you tiptoed on it and slipped, the anointing in the place would cause you to slide from one end of that area to another with great speed and purity. When it was time for me to leave, I wanted to remain there. As I was brought down from the vision, I was brought down through something that appeared to be square and full of beautiful lights.

The next day, I picked up the Bible and it opened to Deut. 4:35 –36 which reads, "Unto thee it was shewed, that thou mightest know that the Lord he is God, there is none else beside him. Out of heaven he made thee to hear his voice that he might instruct thee." I can't describe everything that I saw that night. But I will never forget that experience. Heaven is a real place.

Chapter Nine

The Play

Jesus Christ exposed the mysteries of the biblical book of Revelation to me at a time when my salvation was not complete. God does talk to unsaved people. Paul (previously known as Saul) was not saved when Jesus knocked him to the ground and said, "Saul, Saul, why persecutest thou me?" (Acts 9:4).

The Lord began to deal with me about His coming. I was sitting at work staring out the window and suddenly, I was in a trance. Jesus showed me a group of women sitting on a porch and they were talking about the Lord's coming. God makes things simple. I began to study the scriptures and I recorded the things that God revealed to me about the end times.

The Lord inspired me to write a musical play entitled Raptured/Left Behind, which was performed over 130 times during a twelve year period. He also inspired me to name the group "The Christian Playettes". Our mission was to spread the gospel of Jesus Christ through drama. Our task was to minister to the souls of men and to warn them to be ready for the Rapture.

My older sister was the organist. God anointed my younger sister with a beautiful voice. And, my son was also blessed with an anointed voice. The other members of the cast were family members and wonderful friends – people that God chose from various denominations. The characters were a unique group of people.

One Sunday I visited a nearby church. There was a woman there that was playing the piano during the service. The Lord spoke to me and said, "She is the narrator." I did not know anything about her. I knew other people that attended that church, but I had never met her. After the service, I introduced myself to the God-chosen narrator and asked her if she would like to join the play. Immediately, she accepted. That was God's confirmation. She was a very serious and dedicated Christian. God used her in miraculous ways. Most of us were new Christians but it was very obvious that she had been saved for quite some time. She was filled with the glory of God. The anointing that flowed when she sang brought tears to our eyes.

After the entire cast for the play "Raptured/Left Behind" had been selected, we scheduled rehearsals at my house. During those times, God met us in miraculous ways. He overshadowed us with His presence. The anointing was always very high. We started a prayer requests book and each member of the cast would write their requests in the book. As time passed, we would go through the book and cross out the written requests that God had answered through prayer. We felt very special and knew that God had chosen us for a special work to glorify His name.

God used the narrator in a special way during rehearsals. He would speak through her and He encouraged us and kept us on a high level of the Spirit. We were very happy people. All we wanted to do was to perform the play so that lives would be changed. God opened doors for us to perform in many churches of different denominations. Some of the churches rented a school auditorium in their area. God moved in miraculous ways. There were times when the Power of God flowed around the sanctuary. The Power of God touched the people and we were not able to complete the performance. The Lord filled people with the Holy Ghost during some of the performances.

The cast was very dedicated and they traveled during

inclement weather, through the rain and snow. Nothing could stop their dedication. Of course, we faced many obstacles as we tried to go forth in the will of the Lord, but God sustained us and gave us a determination to go forward. We knew that He had chosen us for a very special work.

We were invited to perform the play at the Community Church of Iselin, which is located in Iselin, New Jersey and is pastored by Elder Arthur L. Jenkins. God completed my salvation there. I am still a member there and I am still being fed with spiritual manna from on high. God's presence fills the sanctuary and He has wrought many miracles there. I've seen people walk in the church with cancer and God healed them. I've also heard people testify that they felt the presence of God when they entered the parking lot. The Community Church is a blessed place.

Chapter Ten

Maybe this is the first time that you're reading about the Rapture. You may also be surprised to read about many things that will take place on the earth as we approach the end times. The things that will occur after the Rapture may also be surprising to you. Surely, Jesus is coming! No one knows the day or the hour but we must be ready to meet the Savior. "Therefore, be ye also ready, for in such an hour as ye think not, the son of man cometh" (Matt. 24:44).

The return of Jesus is certain. Paul has written, "For the Lord himself shall descend from heaven with a shout, with the voice of the archangel, and with the trump of God. Then we which are alive and remain shall be caught up together with them in the clouds to meet the Lord in the air, and so shall we ever be with the Lord" (I Thess. 4:16-17).

The word "Rapture" means caught up! Jesus will return someday soon and the dead in Christ (those believers who are in the graves) and the believers who are alive will instantly be caught up to meet the Lord in midair.

9/11

Most likely no one will ever forget 9/11, the day the terrorists attacked America. On the morning of September 11, 2001, thousands of people left their homes with hope of arriving at their jobs on time and having a usual day at work. However, a short time after 9:00 a.m. that day, their lives were swept away into eternity. None of them had any idea that it would be the last day they would see their loved ones, the last time they would sit at their desks, the last phone call they would make, or the last time that they would attend a meeting.

If the victims of 9/11 had known anything about the terrorists' plans, they would have altered their plans for that day. The coming of Jesus will happen suddenly, just like 9/11. The only difference is that the Christians are looking for His coming, so He will not surprise them. But, to the unsaved, Jesus will appear as a thief in the night.

We must prepare ourselves to meet Jesus. He could come any day. I'll repeat this again: if the people of 9/11 had been informed of a terrorist attack, many of them would have changed their course for that day. Since they did not have that chance, it was too late for them to make other plans. If we are not saved when the Rapture takes place, it will be too late for that trip. There will not be a second chance to make the Rapture.

Signs of the Times – Today's Events

Jesus said that in the last days, nations will rise against other nations. Take a look at the world today. There is always a war going on somewhere on the earth. The Lord also said that there will be famines in the land. Many nations in the world today are filled with people that are starving to death; thousands of them are starving to death daily.

In the end times, pestilences will fill the earth. Read your newspapers – many people have died from being bitten by mosquitoes. A tiny thing as small as a mosquito is causing great fear to fall upon man. It's another fulfillment of prophecy.

The stock market continues to fail. Hundreds of people have lost a lot of money because they invested heavily in the stock market. Some people have committed suicide as a result of their financial losses. This is another sign of the coming of the Lord. Jesus said, "Men's hearts will be failing them for fear and looking at the things which are coming on the earth" (Luke 21:26).

Chapter Eleven

The Trump Will Sound at the Rapture

When the Rapture occurs, the trump will sound and at the last trump, the dead shall be raised incorruptible. When Christians depart this life, they actually fall asleep in Jesus (I. Thess. 4:15-16). The Lord will descend from heaven with a shout. The Christians in the grave will hear the voice of God (John 5:28). The awesome God of the universe will raise them up by His power. Tombstones will be flipped over as the saints are raised from the dirt beneath. The oceans will suddenly be filled with people rising from the bed of the ocean into mid-air to meet Jesus. It doesn't matter how long they've been in the ocean, they will rise. They will be raised up and in a moment, in the twinkling of an eye, they will be changed. The dead will put on incorruption - a body that will never die again; and the living will put on immortality. Their mortal, living bodies will be changed to a body that will never die.

When the Rapture occurs, it will cause chaos on the earth. There will be numerous plane crashes. Christian pilots will suddenly disappear from the airplanes. Every airplane manned by a Christian will immediately take a dive and crash. Every passenger that is filled with the Spirit of God will disappear and be caught up in mid-air to meet the Lord. There will be many trains that will be derailed. Conductors that are filled with the Holy Ghost will suddenly disappear and the materials in their hands will drop to the floor. Christian passengers will suddenly disappear and their seats will be left empty. Unmanned trains will continue with great speeds; many of them will collide.

There will not be anyone left on earth filled with God's

Spirit. Imagine the harsh treatment that the unsaved injured will have to endure. People will have bad attitudes. No one will have a kind word to say to you immediately after the Rapture. Life will be very difficult.

There will probably be millions of car crashes all over the world. Spirit-filled drivers will suddenly disappear, leaving millions of cars in motion without drivers. What disasters! Members of many families will be looking for their loved ones but will not be able to find them. The saved husbands and saved wives will suddenly disappear from the earth. There will be chaos all over the world. Employers will be shocked by the sudden disappearance of their employees.

Unfortunately, there will be many people that are professing Christ that will be left behind. Jesus said, "Two shall be in the field, one taken and the other left; two women shall be grinding at the mill, one taken and the other left" (Matt. 24:41). Don't allow Satan to deceive you. Don't be one of those in the field that is left behind. It will be too late.

Jesus talked about the wise and foolish virgins. The foolish virgins played around and wasted a lot of time. When the bridegroom came, they were not ready. "And while they went to buy, the bridegroom came; and they that were ready went in with him to the marriage: and the door was shut. Afterward came also the other virgins, saying, Lord, Lord open to us. But he answered and said, Verily I say unto you, I know you not. Watch therefore for ye know neither the day nor the hour wherein the Son of man cometh" (Matthew 25:1-10). Notice, the door was shut! It was too late. We cannot afford to be like the foolish virgins.

During Noah's lifetime, the wickedness of man made God

very angry. He decided to destroy man with the flood. Noah and his family entered the ark that God instructed him to build. "And, the Lord shut him in" (Gen. 7:16). When God shuts the door, no one can open it. When the Lord Raptures the church (God's people), I will not report to work that day. I've committed my life to Christ so my secretarial chair will be empty. I will never turn on my computer again. I'm going to be in that number of people that will be "caught up" to meet the Lord in mid-air.

If you haven't made up your mind to live for Christ, do it today! You don't want to be left behind to go through the Tribulation Period. God's salvation plan is found in Acts 2:38, "Repent, and be baptized every one of you in the name of Jesus Christ for the remission of sins, and ye shall receive the gift of the Holy Ghost." Jesus said, "Behold I come quickly" (Rev. 22:7). Prepare yourself to be Rapture ready!

Chapter Twelve

The Scene in Heaven

After the saints are caught up to meet Jesus in mid-air, they will stand before the judgment seat of Christ. They will not stand there to be judged. They were judged at the cross, when Jesus was crucified for the sins of the world. The believers will stand before God to receive their rewards. "For we must all appear before the judgment seat of Christ that every one may receive the things done in his body according to that he hath done, whether it be good or bad" (II Corin. 5:10).

All of the works that we do must glorify the Lord. If we're doing things that God has not given us the authority to do, even though God may be glorified, we will not receive a reward for those works.

The Word of God must authorize our works. "Every man's work shall be made manifest; if any man's work abide which he hath built thereupon he shall receive a reward. If any man's work shall be burned, he shall suffer loss, but he himself shall be saved" (I Corin. 3:14-15).

Awards Ceremony

The scriptures teach us that there will be an *awards ceremony* immediately after the Rapture. The five crowns that will be awarded are:

The Crown of Life – James 1:12

"Blessed is the man that endureth temptation: for when he is tried, he shall receive the crown of life, which the Lord hath promised to them that love him."

29

The Crown of Life will be awarded to those that endure the trials of temptation and tribulations of this life. It is promised to them who love the Lord and look for his appearing and to those who have been faithful and endured to the end (Rev. 2:10; Matt. 24:13).

The Crown of Glory - I Pet. 5:2-4

"Feed the flock of God which is among you, taking the oversight thereof, not by constraint, but willingly; not for filthy lucre, but of a ready mind. Neither as being lords over God's heritage, but being ensamples to the flock. And when the chief Shepherd shall appear, ye shall receive a crown of glory that fadeth not away."

The Crown of Glory is promised to the pastors who faithfully feed God's flock with the truth. It will be given to those pastors who willingly oversee the people of God but not for their own gain, neither overrule God's people, but by being an example to them.

The Crown of Rejoicing - I Thess. 2:19

"For what is our hope, or joy, or crown of rejoicing? Are not even ye in the presence of our Lord Jesus Christ at his coming?"

The Crown of Rejoicing is the "soul winners' crown. It will be given to those who have labored to spread the gospel of Jesus Christ so that souls would hear and receive the gospel of Jesus Christ. Daniel has recorded, "They that turn many to righteousness shall be as the stars for ever and ever" Dan. 12:3.

The Crown of Righteousness - II Tim. 4:8

"Henceforth there is laid up for me a crown of righteousness, which the Lord, the righteous judge, shall give me at that day; and not to me only, but unto all them also that love his appearing."

A Crown of Righteousness will be given to all of the saints because they Love Jesus' appearing. During their time on earth, these people will have lived a righteous life – looking for the return of their Savior.

The Incorruptible Crown - I Corin. 9:25

"And every man that striveth for the mastery is temperate in all things. Now they do it to obtain a corruptible crown; but we an incorruptible."

The Incorruptible Crown will be awarded to those saints who have not yielded their bodies to sin.

Chapter Thirteen

Mansions in Heaven

Jesus promised that He was going away to prepare a place for His people. He said that there are many mansions in heaven. After the saints are raptured, they will occupy their beautiful mansions in glory.

Maybe you have not had the opportunity to occupy a mansion on earth but if you are prepared for the Lord's return, there awaits a mansion for you in heaven – built by God Himself! Imagine occupying something built by God that won't need repairs. The windows will never need to be cleaned. No paint jobs will be needed. It will be absolutely beautiful.

The Marriage Supper

After the awards ceremony that will take place in heaven, the saints will attend the Marriage Supper(Rev. 19:7-9; Rev. 7:9). Christ is the bridegroom; the church (God's people) is the bride and all of His people will be dressed in white linen. Many wonderful things will happen at the marriage supper.

Today is the day of salvation. Prepare yourself to attend the Marriage Supper. The Alleluia Choir will make their first appearance (Rev. 19:6). Maybe you don't sing in a choir in this present life but all of God's people will have a place in the Alleluia Choir. Everybody at the Marriage Supper will be filled with the Holy Ghost. There won't be anyone there causing trouble in the choir. People that have bad attitudes will not be in heaven. No one will argue about what song the choir will sing. God has already decided it. The choir will be a glorious, anointed choir. The Alleluia Choir will sing these words, "Alleluia,

Salvation, and glory, and honor, and power unto the Lord our God" (Rev. 19:1). While the saints are celebrating the Marriage Supper in heaven, there will be a Seven Year Tribulation Period taking place on earth. All of the people that are left behind will have to endure the Tribulation Period.

Chapter Fourteen

The Scene on Earth After the Rapture
The Tribulation Period
Three and One-Half Years of Peace

After the Rapture takes place, the Tribulation Period will begin immediately. It is also known as the "Time of Jacob's Trouble" (Jer. 30:7.) It will be a time when God will deal with the Nation of Israel for rejecting Him as the Messiah. Jesus described it as a time of "great tribulation such as was not since the beginning of the world to this time, no, nor ever shall be" (Matt. 24:21).

After the saints are raptured, it will take some time for the people on earth to understand and accept the fact that many people have suddenly disappeared. This will be a difficult time for them. Some people will remember the times when they heard others talking about the return of the Lord. They'll remember the times when an altar call was given and they refused to allow Jesus to be Lord of their lives. The love of the pleasures of this world that they thought was fulfilling will then become the very thing that will cause them to spend many days and nights in tears. It will take some time for people to recover from the shock that they will experience, as a result of the disappearance of millions of people. The people that will be left behind on earth will continue to live their lives as usual for the first three and one-half years after the Rapture.

The Antichrist

The Antichrist will be revealed. In this present time, he is a mystery. He cannot be revealed before the Rapture takes place (II Thess. 2:8). He will also be known as the Beast and his number is 666 (Rev. 13:18).

The Antichrist will rise up as the world leader. The first three and one-half years of his reign will be peaceful (Dan. 8:24). He will sign a Peace Treaty with Israel and will permit the Jews to offer their daily sacrifices again.

The Witnesses

During that time, the Lord will send two witnesses that will preach the gospel for three and one-half years (Rev. 11:3). Many scholars believe that these two witnesses will be Moses and Elijah. Their witness will be very powerful. God will give them power over their enemies. They will have the power to shut up heaven so that it will not rain. They will be able to turn water to blood and smite the earth with plagues. After evangelizing for three and one-half years, when they have finished their testimony, these two witnesses will be killed. The Antichrist will let their dead bodies lie in the street for three and one-half days. The evil people of that day will rejoice when they hear the news of their deaths. They will send gifts to one another. A grand celebration will be held. The people will be very happy because during these witnesses' days of prophesying, they will torment the evil people because of their wickedness.

After remaining in the street lifeless for three and one-half days, God will put life into the two witnesses and they will stand upon their feet. The people that witness that miracle will be frightened by what their eyes behold. A voice from heaven will speak loud and clear and tell the two witnesses to come up to heaven. Their enemies will watch in awe as they ascend up into the cloud.

The Evangelists

Also, God will seal 144,000 Jews (Rev. 14:4). They will be a special group of people chosen by God to evangelize the

35

world during that period of time. They will preach the word of God. Many people will be saved during the Tribulation Period, but it will cost them their lives - most of them will be martyrs. The people that will be left behind on earth will be warned not to take the mark of the Beast (Rev. 14:9).

Chapter Fifteen

Three and One-Half Years of Trouble (Dan. 9:27)

At the end of the three and one-half years of peace, the Antichrist will turn on the people. He will go into the temple, sit there and claim to be God (II Thess. 2:4.). Isn't that just like the devil? During Paul's missionary journey to Corinth, he told the Corinthians, "And no marvel for Satan himself is transformed into an angel of light." The Antichrist will take control of the whole world. He will be given power over all kindreds, and tongues, and nations (Rev. 13:7). Many people will worship him.

The False Prophet

The Antichrist will have an assistant, the False Prophet. He will have the ability to exercise the same power as the Antichrist. Among the many things that he will be able to do will be to call down fire from heaven. Many people will be deceived as a result of the miracles that he will perform.

This is one of the reasons why we should not be carried away with people in the world today that are exercising gifts. Many of them are using their gifts for self-gain instead of allowing God to work through them to use the gifts for His glory. Our spirit will bear witness with their spirit if a person is operating under the divine inspiration of the Lord. "Beloved, believe not every spirit, but try the spirits whether they are of God; because many false prophets are gone out into the world" (I John 4:1).

The Mark of the Beast

The Antichrist will have demon-filled employees working

for him day and night. They will set up stations to give out the mark of the Beast. People will be deceived and will take his mark on the right hand or the forehead (Rev. 13:16). This will be his means of controlling the entire world. If you take the mark of the Beast, it means you have sold your soul to the devil and you will spend eternity in the Lake of Fire. John described it as torment in the Lake of Fire forever (Rev. 14:10). There will not be anyone to supply you with water to cool your soul. It will be an eternal life of pain and torture.

Those who are left to endure the Tribulation Period and choose not to receive the mark of the Beast will not be able to buy or sell anything – absolutely nothing! You will not be able to purchase medicine. Imagine! If you have certain medications that you must take on a daily basis, you will not be able to get refills without the mark of the Beast on your forehead or on your right hand. The suffering will be absolutely unbearable. Suppose you wear glasses, you will not be able to get them changed. How will you manage to see? How will you get around? You won't be able to drive a car without the proper vision. You won't be able to walk around in your own house if you can't see. Most likely, the Antichrist will take your home and his demonic employees will take up residence there. You will not be able to purchase food without the mark of the Antichrist. Many people will spend a lot of days starving and crying due to hunger pains.

Suppose you own a business. Your money will not be of any value to you during the Tribulation Period if you do not take the mark of the Beast. Your business could be the most prosperous business in the world right now. The Antichrist will shut it down. You won't be able to sell anything. Nothing! Absolutely nothing! All of your lifetime savings will no longer belong to you. The Antichrist will control the banks. Only the people with his mark will have access to their accounts. And as for those people, their destiny will be the Lake of Fire.

Chapter Sixteen

Credit Cards

Recently, I was shopping at one of the local department stores. When I finished putting all of the items that I needed into the cart, I proceeded to the checkout.
The cashier scanned all of the items and then she scanned my credit card. The system would not process the charge. I knew that I had enough availability on the credit card to cover the charge and I assured the clerk that there was no reason for the denial. At that moment, I could feel my heart starting to beat faster. Negative thoughts rushed to my mind. For about two minutes, I stood there fighting those thoughts. The clerk tried to process the card one more time and it was cleared. She discovered that there was a problem with the store's system. I sighed with relief. All I could say was, "Thank you Jesus!"

As I walked out of the store, my mind reflected on the coming Tribulation Period. I imagined the state of panic that will be present when people try to use their bankcards and they won't be processed if the people don't have the mark of the Beast on the right hand or the forehead. Life will be extremely difficult during that time.

So, I am pleading with you - if you are not saved, make a decision right now to accept Jesus Christ as Lord of your life. Right where you are, ask Jesus to fill you with His Spirit. Without His Spirit, you cannot be raptured. "Now if any man have not the Spirit of Christ, he is none of his" (Romans 8:9).

Today is the day of salvation. You may say that you're not ready and that you don't think you can make the commitment to serve Christ now. Why not? Give Christ a chance. Through Christ, you can do all things. "Yea, I will help thee," saith the Lord (Isa. 41:10).

The people who receive Jesus Christ as their Savior and refuse to take the mark of the Beast during that time will be beheaded (Rev.20:4). They will be forced to lay their heads on chopping blocks and the axe will come down! Think of that! Having your head chopped off for accepting Christ. Daniel lived many years before John came on the scene. God revealed to Daniel that the Antichrist will arise and that he will wear out the saints saved during the Tribulation Period (Dan. 7:25; Rev. 13:7.). The nation of Israel has been blinded during this present period of Grace because of their refusal to accept Jesus Christ as their Messiah (Rom. 11:25).

God has extended an invitation to all of us to become His sons. Take advantage of it today. Don't wait until the door is closed. The nation of Israel's eyes will be opened during the reign of the Antichrist but what a price they will have to pay for accepting Christ during that time.

Chapter Seventeen

The Wrath of God During the Tribulation Period

God is a God of love. His mercy endureth forever. But the wickedness of man makes God angry. During the Tribulation Period, God will pour out His wrath upon the earth. It is not known at what point the following events will occur, but they will happen as written by John in the book of Revelation.

Earthquakes and Plagues

There will be a great earthquake that will take place during that period of time. Seven thousand people will die as a result of the earthquake (Rev. 11:13). Houses will disappear. Buildings will be shaken and fall to the ground. Hundreds of pieces of glass will be falling from broken windows. Large bricks will fall to the ground as buildings crumble; most likely the impact will kill many people that will be hit by them.

Great men, rich men, and mighty men will be asking the mountains and rocks to fall on them and to hide them from the face of God and from the great wrath of the Lamb of God (Rev. 6:16). God will plague the wicked people with sores (Rev. 16:2). Boils will cover their bodies. They will not be able to get any relief from the plague. Think about it! Boils will become infected and begin to drain and probably will cause much pain. God showed His power during the Israelites' struggle to leave Egypt and escape bondage. Again, He will send plagues upon the earth.

The Bottomless Pit

The bottomless pit will be opened and a great smoke will come up. Locusts will come out of the smoke. The locusts will have faces like men. Their hair will look like women's hair. Their teeth will be like the teeth of lions. Their bodies will be shaped like horses. They will have tails like scorpions and they will use them to sting the people that are left behind. These locust-like creatures will be given the power to torment the people on earth for a period of five months. And, during that five month period, you will not be able to die. Death will flee from you (Rev. 9). Imagine being tormented to the point of death and not being able to die. God will not allow death to take over.

Funeral homes will be closed for a period of five months because no one will be requesting their services. If you jump from the tallest building in the world, you'll still be well alive with no broken bones when you land on the ground. Suicide will not be in effect during that five-month period. It will have no power. God will command death to "take a walk for five months."

Suppose there is a knock at the door and, upon answering, you open the door to find one of the locusts standing there. You won't be able to escape those creatures. They will be roaming around all over the world. Millions of them will fill the earth. If you are left behind, how will you manage to sleep? It will probably be very difficult to do so.

Chapter Eighteen

More Wrath

An army of thousands will ride horses; the heads of the horses will look like heads of lions. These creatures will be able to open their mouths and out of their mouths will come smoke, fire and brimstone. The pain and torture that they will cause will make it very difficult for mankind to endure.

God created the Sun to provide a light for us in the day. However, during the Tribulation Period when God will punish man for his wickedness, He will use this same Sun that provides light for you today, to scorch you (Rev. 16:8). It will be too hot to walk outside. The heat from the Sun will burn human flesh as people stand on the streets. The smell of burning human flesh will be present. Very often now, we hear news of the ozone layer disappearing. This process has to occur. During the Tribulation Period the ozone layer will be completely removed which will cause the Sun to become hotter so that it can perform the task of punishment that God will command it to do.

The Hail Plague

God will plague the earth with hail. Hail weighing approximately 130 pounds will fall upon the earth (Rev. 16:21). Imagine the weight of the hail that will be falling from the sky and hitting people on the head. Some people will suffer great injuries and some of them will die from the impact caused by the falling hail. When Pharaoh refused to allow the children of Israel to leave Egypt, the Lord rained hail upon the land of Egypt. It destroyed man and beast. Trees were broken in half during that plague (Exodus 9:24). God will repeat His actions during the Tribulation Period. The suffering will be great and it will be the result of the wickedness of men.

The Sea Turned To Blood

The sea will be turned into blood. Imagine turning on your faucet to get a cold drink of water. Instead of seeing running water, you will see running blood. The fish and all living creatures in the sea will die (Rev. 8:8). You won't be able to have fish for dinner. They will no longer exist during that time.

Then suddenly a star named Wormwood will fall from heaven and cause the waters to become bitter. Men will die because of the bitterness of the waters. Although God will send the plagues upon the earth, the people of that day will continue to murder, fornicate and steal (Rev. 9:21). Satan will have control of the land.

Chapter Nineteen

Armageddon

Towards the end of the Tribulation Period, there will be a battle that I will call "the battle of battles." It will be the Battle of Armageddon, which will be created by God (Rev. 16:16; Zech 14: Zech. 12, Joel 3:12). God will draw the nations into the valley of Jehoshaphat to fight against Israel because of their rejection of Him as their Messiah and their disobedience.

This will be one of the worst battles ever fought on this earth. Thousands of people will die in the Battle of Armageddon. Human blood will be in the streets as high as horses' bridles (Rev. 14:20). There will be dead bodies everywhere. It will take seven months to bury the dead people (Ezek. 39:11-12; Rev. 6:15-17). The fowls of the air will be called to a supper and they will eat the dead bodies of those killed during the battle of Armageddon (Rev. 19:17-18).

Christ Returns to Earth

As King of Kings

After Jesus' resurrection, He remained on earth for forty days. He assembled His disciples together and gave them instructions concerning the Kingdom of God. Suddenly, He was taken up and a cloud received Him. The disciples stood there, watching in amazement as He ascended. Two men stood there and asked the disciples, "Why stand ye gazing up into heaven? This same Jesus which is taken up from you into heaven shall so come in like manner as ye have seen him go into heaven."

At the end of the Tribulation Period, Jesus Christ will

return to the earth as King of Kings and Lord of Lords and He will end the Battle of Armageddon (Rev. 19:16). He will descend to the Mount of Olives that faces Jerusalem on the east, as promised (Zech. 14:4). He will stand there and the Mount of Olives will cleave in the middle. As a result of the impact and God's power, it will create a very great valley. One part of the mountain will move to the north and the other half of it will move toward the south.

"For if we believe that Jesus died and rose again, even so them also which sleep in Jesus will God bring with him" (I Thess. 4:14). The saints that are raptured will return to the earth with Christ, in their glorified bodies (Zech. 14:5; Rev. 19:14). They will be clothed in fine white linen. The white linen represents the righteousness of the saints.

When the nation of Israel sees Christ upon His return with the prints in His hands, they will be saved. The scriptures teach us that Israel will be saved in a day. The multitude that survives the battle of Armageddon will see and acknowledge that Jesus Christ is the Messiah (Rom. 11:26; Zech. 12:10). Jesus Christ will cast the Antichrist and his assistant, the False Prophet, into the Lake of Fire that will be burning with brimstone.

Satan Bound

The Lord will send an angel from heaven that will have the key to the bottomless pit. He will lay hold on Satan, otherwise known as the Devil. The angel will bind him and cast him into the Bottomless Pit where he will remain locked up for 1,000 years.

Judgment of Nations

The nations that survive the Battle of Armageddon will be

called to the Judgment of the Nations, which will include the nations that fight against Israel in that Battle. Although God will use them to punish his people, He will punish the nations that fight against Israel.) Their punishment will be severe. Their eyes will consume away in their sockets; their flesh will fall from their bones as they stand upon their feet (Zech. 14; Joel 3:2).

Chapter Twenty

The Millennium Reign

Before Jesus' crucifixion, the disciples thought that He had arrived on earth to set up His Kingdom. However, His Kingdom will be established during the Millennium. Millennium means 1,000 years. Jesus will set up his earthly Kingdom in Jerusalem and since Satan will be bound in the bottomless pit during that time, there will be peace on earth for 1,000 years (Rev. 20:7).

All of the saints that will be killed during the Tribulation Period (by the Antichrist's orders) will be raised from the dead to live during the Millennium (Rev. 20:4) along with the Raptured Saints that will come back to earth with Jesus in their glorified bodies (Zech. 14:5).

Israel will rebuild its nation as recorded in Isaiah 65:21. The saints will rule the earth (I Corin. 6:2). The believers will be the town officers. It will be a time of peace when the lamb and the wolf will feed together (Isaiah 65:25). Every animal will be tamed. There will be no need to lock the doors at night. No one will be intruding. The peace of Christ will rule the land.

At the end of the Millennium (1,000 years), Satan will be loosed for a short season to gather an army from the people who will survive the Tribulation Period and enter the Millennium Period. Certainly, during the 1,000-year period, many children will be born. They will grow up and they will have an opportunity to accept Christ or reject him and join Satan. Christ does not force anyone to serve Him. It's a choice.

Chapter Twenty-One

The Battle of Gog and Magog

After Satan is released from the Bottomless Pit, he will succeed in gathering an army to battle Christ and the saints. The battle will be called the Battle of Gog & Magog (Rev. 20:8). As Satan and his army surrounds the saints' camp, God will send down fire from heaven and consume them. He will cast Satan into the Lake of Fire (Rev. 20:10).

It's amazing that Satan would attempt to come against God. The Psalmist made it very clear when he penned Psalm 33:8, "Let all the earth fear the Lord; let all the inhabitants of the world stand in awe of him. For he spake, and it was done; he commanded, and it stood fast. The Lord bringeth the counsel of the heathen to nought; he makes the devices of the people of none effect." Why would anyone put his or her trust in Satan?

Chapter Twenty-Two

Great White Throne Judgment

After the Battle of Gog and Magog, Christ will sit on the throne of judgment. Those who died unsaved will be resurrected from the dead to stand before God at the Great White Throne Judgment. The sea will give up the dead. All of the unsaved people that have been cremated and cast into the sea, and those that were unsaved and lost their lives in the sea and were never found, will, by the power of God, be raised in a bodily form to stand before God (Rev. 20:12).

"For we must all appear before the judgment seat of Christ; that every one may receive the things done in his body, according to that he hath done, whether it be good or bad" (II Corin. 5:10).

The Books Will Be Opened

The books will be opened and the Book of Life will be opened. Those whose names are not written in the Book of Life will be cast into the Lake of Fire that burneth with fire and brimstone.

The Bible lists some of the kinds of people that will be cast into the Lake of Fire. Among them will be the fearful. "God has not given us a spirit of fear, but one of power, love, and a sound mind." The people that allow fear to overtake them will be drawn of their own lust. When lust is conceived, it bringeth forth sin. And sin bringeth forth death! A lack of trusting God will lead to trusting in the things of this world. The fearful and haters will be cast into the Lake of Fire. The Bible declares that we cannot love God whom we have not seen, and at the same time hate our brothers whom we have seen. Hatred comes from the

51

devil. God is love. When He comes into your life, He brings love. All liars will be cast into the Lake of Fire. Lying is from the devil. Jesus Christ is Truth. When Christ is Lord of your life, you will speak the truth. All sorcerers, drug users and those involved in witchcraft that have not repented will stand before God and their destiny will be the Lake of Fire.

Jesus Christ can deliver you from drugs; but if you do not repent and make him Lord of your life, you will spend Eternity in flames. All murderers will be cast into the Lake of Fire. If you have committed murder, ask God to forgive you and allow Him to fill you with His Spirit. If you fail to do so and die unsaved, the Lake of Fire will be your home forever.

When we think of the word "murder", most of us think of killing another person with some type of weapon. But that is not the only means of murder. We can also destroy people with our tongue. It is a weapon. James has written that the tongue is a fire, an unruly evil, and full of deadly poison. Imagine going to hell as a result of improper use of our tongue. Murderers and liars that have not repented and made Jesus Lord of their lives will not be in heaven.

Many people have had to endure some difficult times because of something that someone else said. God has instructed us to be swift to hear and slow to speak. I am reminded of what Jesus said in Matthew 12:36, "But I say unto you, that every idle word that men shall speak, they shall give account thereof in the Day of Judgment. For by thy words thou shalt be justified, and by thy words thou shalt be condemned." My prayer is that God will season my speech so that I will not be found guilty of destroying my friends, my family, or my enemies by using my tongue inappropriately.

Chapter Twenty-Three

Life In the Lake of Fire

There will be weeping and gnashing of teeth in the Lake of Fire. Imagine yourself in the pit of hell, with fire burning all around you, people screaming from the pain. The people that choose the Lake of Fire to be their eternal dwelling place will be crying tears that will never dry; gnashing of the teeth will be heard everywhere and forever!

The sad part about this is that we will never see the unsaved people again. Our friends and family members that die unsaved will be separated from the believers for eternity. If we are saved, we have an obligation to witness to our friends, family members and enemies about the coming of the Lord Jesus Christ. We can't let Jesus down by failing to do so.

If the house was on fire and we knew that there were people inside, we would do all that we could to get them out. Our concern for souls should be greater. The Lake of Fire is real. Let's do all that we can to witness to our family, friends and enemies about the saving grace of Jesus Christ.

Chapter Twenty-Four

Eternity for the Christians

This present heaven and earth will be destroyed with fire. "The heaven and the earth, which are now, by the same word are kept in store, reserved unto fire against the day of judgment and perdition of ungodly men" (II Peter 3:12). The scriptures teach us that in the day of the Lord, the heavens will be on fire, dissolved, and the elements shall melt with fervent heat. God is going to create a new heaven and a new earth (Rev. 21:1). Nothing unclean will walk in them.

Jesus Christ is going to wipe away all tears from the Christians' eyes. They will never cry again, they will never have any more pain, and all of the things that they have suffered will be forgotten. This present world and the events that take place in it will never come into their minds again (Isaiah 65:17). John described the New Jerusalem that God showed him in a vision. The streets will be paved with gold. In this present day, sometimes it seems as though only the rich people have a lot of gold. If you're a Christian and make the Rapture, don't worry – you will walk on gold. God said so! There will be a pure river of water of life that will proceed out of the throne of God. There will also be a tree of life there, which will bear twelve kinds of fruits. The leaves of it will be for the healing of the nations.

So shall we ever be with the Lord!

Chapter Twenty-Five

In this chapter, I have included a step-by-step outline of the events that will take place at the time of the Rapture and thereafter.

The Rapture
Jesus will return to rapture the saints. Rapture means caught up! For the Lord himself shall descend from heaven with a shout, with the voice of the archangel and with the trump of God (IThess.4:16). In a moment, in the twinkling of an eye, we shall be changed – the dead will put on incorruption, the living will put on immortality. At the last trump, for the trumpet shall sound and the dead shall be raised incorruptible (I Corin. 15:51); the dead in Christ shall rise first and we which are alive and remain shall be caught up with them to meet the Lord in the air (I Thess.4:16). Two shall be in the field, one taken and the other left, two women shall be grinding at the mill, one taken and the other left (Matt. 24:40).

When the saints are raptured, they will appear before the Judgment Seat of Christ for Spiritual Rewards – II Corin.5:10 Crowns Awarded: Life – James 1:12; Glory IPet.5:2-4; Rejoicing – I Thes. 2:19; Righteousness II Tim.4:8; Incorruptible I Corin.9:25.

Marriage Supper takes place – 7-year period – (Rev. 19:7-9; Rev.7:9). Christ is the bridegroom; the Church is the bride dressed in white Linen.

The Allelujah Choir will sing – Rev. 19:6, Saints will occupy mansions – John 14:2. Those believers of the Old and New Testament that died before Jesus went to Calvary and the Church began are those that are Called to the Marriage Supper of Jesus the bridegroom and the Church his bride (Rev. 19:9)

The Tribulation Period of 7 Years will begin on earth immediately following the Rapture. It is also known as the Time of Jacob's Trouble (Jer. 30:7). God's dealings with the Nation of Israel for rejecting Him as the Messiah.

The Tribulation Period
3 ½ Yrs. Peace -Dan. 8:24; 9:27 - The Antichrist (also known as the Beast – His number is 666) Rev. 13 – He arises and signs a Peace Treaty with Israel – Allows them to offer sacrifices again.

God will send two witnesses to the earth and they will preach 3 1/2yrs (Rev. 11:3). People will be warned not to take the Mark of the Beast – Rev. 14:9. 144,000 Jews will be sealed (Rev. 14:4) – they are a special group of Jews from the twelve tribes of Israel that will be sealed by God. They will evangelize the world!

3 ½ Years Later – This will be 3 ½ years of trouble - Dan. 9:27. The Antichrist's demonic nature will be revealed. He will go into the temple and set himself of as God (IIThess.2:4). He will begin to give out the Mark of the Beast on the right hand or the forehead (Rev. 13:16). The Antichrist will wear out the saints that are saved during the Tribulation Period – Dan. 7:25; Rev. 13:7. If you don't take the Mark, you will not be able to buy nor sell anything – absolutely nothing – no medicine, food, NOTHING! (Rev.13:16-17).

Those who refuse to take the Mark will have their heads chopped off for Jesus' sake (Rev. 20:4). If you take the mark, you will be tormented in the Lake of Fire forever (Rev. 14:10).

During the Tribulation Period, God will pour out his wrath upon the earth because of man's disobedience and refusal to accept him as Lord: Earthquake – 7,000 people will die (Rev. 11:13). Sores will cover people's bodies - Rev. 16:2; Locusts with faces like men and hair like women, and teeth like lions will torment people for 5 months. They will seek death but will not be able to die. Funeral homes will be closed for 5 months. The Sun will scorch the people (Rev. 16:8). Hell weighing 100lbs. will fall upon the earth – Rev. 16:21. Water will be turned to blood – Rev. 8:8. It is not clear during what period during the Tribulation Period that God will pour out his wrath upon the earth, but it will happen.

The Battle of Armageddon Created by God will take place (Rev, 16:16; Zech. 14; Zech. 12; Joel 3:12). God will draw nations into valley of Jehoshaphat to fight Israel because of their rejection of him and disobedience. Blood will be in the streets as high as horses' bridles (Rev. 14:20. It will take 7 months to bury the dead Ezek. 39:11-12; Rev.6:15-17. Fowls will eat their bodies (Rev. 19:17-18).

Christ will return to earth as King of Kings. Jesus will return to Mt. Olives – Acts. 1:11; Zech. 14:4. The Raptured and Old Testament saints will return with him – Zach 14:5. The Israelites will see prints in Jesus' hands Zech. 12:10. Jesus will end the Battle of Armageddon. He will rule as King of Kings and Lord of Lords – Rev. 19:16. Jesus will cast the Antichrist and False Prophet into the Lake of Fire alive – Rev. 19:20. Those who took the mark of the beast will be slain by Jesus – Rev. 19:21. Satan will be locked up for 1,000 years – Rev. 20:3.

Judgment of the Nations will take place. The nations that fight against Israel in the Battle of Armageddon will be called to the Judgment of the Nations. Though God will use them to punish his people, He will punish those nations for fighting against Israel. Their eyes will consume away in their sockets, their flesh will fall from their bones as they stand upon their feet – Zech. 14, Joel 3:2. This will also be the time when Jesus will separate the sheep from the goats. The sheep (gentile nations that are saved) will enter the Millennium Kingdom. The goats (gentile nations that are wicked didn't visit his people in prison, nor visit seek or feed hungry during Tribulation Period will be cast into the Lake of Fire (Matt. 25:31).

Christ Will Set Up His Kingdom. It is called the Millennium Reign. Jesus Christ will rule as King in Jerusalem – There will be 1,000 years of peace (known as the Kingdom Age). Christ will set up His Kingdom in Jerusalem – Rev. 20. The Saints killed during the Tribulation Period (by the Antichrist's orders) will be raised from the dead to live during that time (Rev.20:4; Dan.12:2) along with the Raptured and Old Testament Saints who come to earth with Jesus in their glorified bodies (Zech.14:5). Also, the people that survive the Tribulation Period and have not served the Antichrist will enter the Kingdom Age. Israel will rebuild – Isaiah 65:21. Saints will rule the earth (I Corin.6:2). The lamb and the wolf will feed together – Isaiah 65:25. There will be total piece during the Millennium.

At the end of the 1,000 years, Satan will be loosed for a short season – Millennial people (in their natural bodies – that either survived the Tribulation Period or are born during the 1,000 years) will have a chance to serve Christ eternally or reject him and join Satan. Unfortunately, there will be people that will join Satan in a battle against God and his people. It is called the Battle of God & Magog – Rev. 20:8 – Created by Satan. Satan will gather an army against the saints. God will send down fire from heaven and consume them and Christ will cast Satan into the Lake of Fire – Rev. 20:10. The devil will be destroyed.

Then God will sit at the Great White Throne Judgment. Those people who died unsaved will be resurrected from the dead to stand before God at the Great White Throne Judgment along with those who join Satan during the short period he rules after the Millennium. They will have to give an account of the deeds done in their bodies. There is a record of our lives being kept. The Books will be opened. The Fearful, Haters, Liars, Sorcerers, and Murderers will be cast into the Lake of fire for Eternity – Rev. 20:11.

This present Heaven and Earth will be destroyed 2Peter 3:12. God will create a New Heaven and a New Earth. Rev. 21:1. This present world and the events that take place in it will never come into our minds again (Isaiah 65:17). There will be no more crying nor pain – Rev. 21. So shall we ever be with the Lord!

Helen V. Alexander

Books by Helen V. Alexander

A Daily Word From God

Sunday School Lessons

Prayers – 365 Daily Prayers & Decrees

Rapture

Made in the USA
Columbia, SC
18 April 2018